The Story of Flight

Contents

★   ★   ★

You can find more information about names and
words marked with an * beginning on page 33.
This shape, ❑, shows you where a sticker goes.

Leonardo da Vinci began his studies on bird flight in 1486. ▶

People

have dreamed

about flying for thousands

of years. They've told stories

about flying gods, flying animals, even

flying carpets. According to Greek legend,

Icarus flew on wax-and-feather

wings. Some people tried to make dreams of

flying real. **Leonardo da Vinci*** designed **fly-**

ing machines in the 15th century. Now

scientists are working on jet packs for fly-

ing in space. And stories about flying people, like

Superman and other superheroes, are still popular.

Pieter Brueghel the Elder, *Landscape with the Fall of Icarus* (detail), 1553–1562

Thomas Walker, an English portrait painter, designed a flying machine with flapping wings in 1816. ❏ ▶

Francesco de Lana-Terzi's flying ship (1670)

Birdman

The strange-looking machine to the left was built by Reuben J. Spaulding in 1889. It never flew. Human chest muscles are not strong enough to flap a pair of wings to fly.

Brilliant Bird-Watcher

Leonardo da Vinci analyzed bird flight; he studied bird bones and muscles. Then he designed a wing with several movable joints connected to a complex series of springs. Da Vinci created over 500 flight designs, including drawings for a propeller, a helicopter, even a parachute — and he did it nearly 500 years ago! None of Da Vinci's flying machines actually took off, but his ideas were influential.

A Flying Ship

In the 17th century, Francesco de Lana-Terzi planned to suspend a ship from four huge copper balls. He thought if he then pumped all of the air out of the balls, the ship would float up. The airless metal balls really would have burst in the atmosphere. But the idea was right: A machine lighter than air *will* rise.

This 1905 French cartoon shows the kind of airmail delivery expected by the year 2000.

A jointed, flapping wing built according to Da Vinci's sketch

Jacob Degen's flying machine (1807). The balloon* that lifts it is not shown. ▶

Airborne Animals

Birds. Insects. Mammals. Reptiles. Fish. Some of them might be airborne, but can they really *fly*? Most **birds*** fly using a flapping wing motion. Many **insects*** also fly. Some mammals, such as **bats**, are amazing fliers. Other animals just appear to fly. They don't **propel*** or move themselves through the air like birds; they **glide*** on air currents. Some lizards, frogs, and squirrels have skin flaps that spread out like wings for gliding. A flying snake flattens itself to glide from a tree. Flying fish flap their tails to push themselves out of the water, then spread their fins like fans to glide.

Pteranodon: This prehistoric flying reptile had a wingspan of 27 feet.

▲ A fly beats its wings 200 times per second, making a figure-eight pattern with every beat.

Some flying fish can glide for nearly 1,600 feet! ▼

4

In these imaginary landscapes, you will find real animals: birds from different countries,

bats that are flying, mammals, amphibians, and reptiles that are gliding, and

flying insects like butterflies, beetles, and bees. *See* page 42 for the names of these airborne animals.

On the Wing

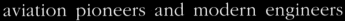

Early aviation pioneers and modern engineers have learned much about flight by observing birds. Birds are **aerodynamic***: They move easily through the air. Wing shape and movement help birds stay aloft and move forward.

▲ A parrot in flight

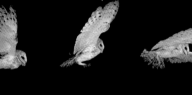

▲ A barn owl, like other birds, flaps its wings up, down, and forward.

The upper surface of a bird's wing is curved, while the lower surface is flat. Air flows quickly over the top of the wing; it flows slower underneath. The difference or **lift*** helps the bird fly. When birds take flight, their feet fold back; when they land, their feet come forward. Tail feathers* help birds steer or brake.

An albatross may have a 12-foot wingspan. This bird can glide for hours. It can even sleep while flying!

This plane moves because wings support it in the air and propellers pull it forward. Birds flap their wings to do the same thing. ▶

The wing of a buzzard, a type of North American vulture

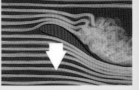

Buzzard

Wings

Birds can raise one wing tip and lower the other at the same time. This helps them balance in air currents.

Movement

Birds can fly or glide. They can tip their wings to slow down and land. To hover over the same spot, birds lower their tail feathers and beat their wings quickly.

Feathers

Feathers help a bird control its flight pattern. The wing feathers overlap and can be folded together, spread apart, or turned. Feathers are used on arrows to make them fly straight.

A peregrine falcon in flight. It can dive at over 200 mph!

Lift and Drag

Air flows faster *over* a bird's wings. It has a lower pressure* than the slower-moving, higher-pressure air flowing *under* the bird's wings. Lift is created by this difference in air pressure. Air isn't just flowing over and under the wings—it's also pushing against the bird. This creates a braking force known as drag*. All aircraft are affected by lift and drag.

▲ A peregrine falcon wing

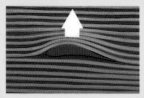

◄ The different action of air flowing over and under a wing produces lift.

When a wing angles, the air flow changes. Lift is reduced; flight is stalled*. ▶

Riding the Wind

Kites are among the oldest airborne machines. When a kite is pulled against the wind, it rises. The kite will stay up as long as the pull on its string equals the force of the wind lifting the kite. **Gliders*** also use the wind. Unlike airplanes, they have no engines. But like kites, gliders are pulled up into the air, usually by an airplane. When they are released, they **glide** on air currents, the same way birds sometimes do. At the same time, gravity's pull causes the glider to **descend*** slowly.

Warm currents of air or thermals* help keep a glider aloft. Glider pilots must monitor air currents closely if they want to glide for long distances.

A parachute traps air in its canopy, which slows its fall. ⌐

Flying Objects

No one knows when Australian Aborigines first threw boomerangs, some of the earliest flying objects. Kites were invented by the Chinese over 2,000 years ago. Marco Polo brought the news to Europeans in the 13th century. Kites have been used for war, science, and amusement. One of the most famous U.S. kite fliers was Benjamin Franklin. He used a kite to study electricity in the 1750s.

Gliders

After kites and boomerangs, gliders are the simplest type of heavier-than-air aircraft. The first real human flight probably took place in 1852 in a three-winged glider designed by Sir George Cayley*.

Parachutes

Chinese acrobats may have used parachutes in the 1300s. Leonardo da Vinci's parachute sketches dated from 1485. But it was the 18th-century French who coined the word from *parare* (shield) and *chute* (fall), and made the first real parachute descents. In 1797, André-Jacques Garnerin wore one and jumped from a balloon flying over 2,500 feet high. He was the first to use parachutes often and with success. For most of World War I (1914–1918), military balloonists wore parachutes, but pilots didn't. Parachutes weren't considered useful with airplanes. Parachutes were once made from canvas or silk; now they are made from a variety of strong artificial fabrics.

Happy Landings

A person free-falling at a speed of 50 yards per second will gradually slow to a

5-yards-per-second fall wearing a parachute. The parachutist slows down until the force of the air rising against the parachute nearly equals the force of gravity pulling it down. Then the parachutist descends at a steady slow rate. Parachutes are sometimes used to brake jet planes.

JPC

Balloons

On November 21, 1783, an astonished crowd in France stared into the sky as the world's first passenger balloon floated by. Among the crowd were the balloon's creators, **Joseph-Michel** and **Jacques-Etienne Montgolfier***. Joseph-Michel thought smoke made things rise. He decided to capture smoke in a balloon to make it ascend*. He thought the worst-smelling smoke would work best, so he burned old shoes, wool, and spoiled meat. The inventor didn't realize it was heat that expanded the air and caused the balloon to rise. The Montgolfier brothers built a cloth balloon or **aerostat*** seven stories high for the November launch.

Balloon filled with helium*

Balloons drift wherever the winds carry them.

Early aeronauts'* control equipment: an anchor to secure the balloon and ballast* for weight. When ballast was thrown off, the balloon rose. ❑

A gondola is a wicker or aluminum basket. In modern hot-air balloons, it holds propane burners.

The Montgolfiers' passenger balloon was released in a royal garden near Paris. It stayed in the air for 25 minutes before landing about six miles away.

A "fire-box" hung from the balloon's open neck. The aeronauts stoked the fire to control the altitude* or flying height.

Dirigibles

Braz. Santos-. dirigible circled the Eiffel Tower in 1901.

The **airship*** was invented in France in 1852 by Henri Giffard. Like a balloon, an airship stays up because it's filled with lighter-than-air gas. But unlike a balloon, an airship is powered. Engines turn propellers that move the airship forward. Pilots can steer using **rudders**. In the 1920s and 1930s, giant hydrogen*-filled airships or **dirigibles*** carried the first passengers across the Atlantic Ocean.

The *Graf Zeppelin*, built in Germany in 1928, was almost 775 feet long — more than two-and-a-half football fields end to end! Here is the *Graf Zeppelin* seen from below ▶ and from the side.▼

Modern blimps* are filled with helium, which does not burn. □

Life on Board

A dirigible's gondola had a pilot's cabin, a navigation station, a cabin for the crew, passenger cabins, a kitchen, and a dining room. The average time for a zeppelin flight from Germany to the United States was 110 hours.

Zeppelins

The most famous airship maker was German, Count Ferdinand von Zeppelin*. He started building rigid dirigibles in 1900. The first zeppelins traveled under 37 mph. Their outsides were painted to reflect the sun. This kept the gas inside from getting too hot and exploding.

Mooring

There was a dirigible mooring mast on the Empire State Building in New York City. It never worked because of strong wind updrafts.

Disaster

The *Hindenburg* was the largest zeppelin ever built. On May 6, 1937, the giant hydrogen airship burst into flames mooring in Lakehurst, New Jersey. 36 of the over 100 people on board were killed.

▲ The 800-foot *Hindenburg* was destroyed in less than a minute.

◄ Gondola

A rigid dirigible has a light metal skeleton that supports a network of metal wires. The crew moves around on metal catwalks. A nonrigid airship, or blimp, doesn't have this skeleton.

Inside a dirigible, hydrogen was kept in separate sections. This helped prevent leaks of the flammable gas. ▼

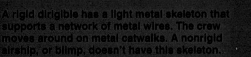

Gliders and Planes Take Off!

Otto Lilienthal's gliders were inspired by his bird studies.

Design for one of Lilienthal's gliders ▶

Otto Lilienthal's* work with glid-

ers showed how flight could be controlled.

Meanwhile, **Clément Ader*** was building aircraft that

were powered. Modern **aviation**—controlled and pow-

ered flight—began to take off. Lilienthal built several gliders with folding

wings in the 1890s. He made over 2,000 flights in his gliders. Lilienthal

took each glider to a hilltop and got inside. He gripped his

glider with his elbows and started running against the wind.

Man and glider lifted into the air. Lilienthal controlled his craft

by shifting his weight. He was the first flier ever photographed.

▲ Otto Lilienthal

One of Clément Ader's planes was modeled after the Australian flying fox, a type of bat.

Design for the *Eole*, the plane built by Ader in 1890, which flew 165 feet ▶

Lilienthal's gliders were made of bamboo covered by light cloth.
Some had a single pair of wings; some had two pairs.

Batman

Clément Ader was also at work in the 1890s. One of his flying machines was shaped like a giant bat. Ader's plane was not a glider. It had a steam engine* that turned a propeller. The propeller gave the plane power, so it moved through, not just glided on, the air. Ader was able to take off in his bat plane, but wasn't able to control it after that.

U.S. Inventors

Lilienthal's experiments inspired U.S. engineer Octave Chanute* to add springs to his glider wings. This made the wings rock, not break, in strong winds. Samuel Pierpont Langley* flew large model planes that used an engine, twin propellers, and two pair of curved wings. His piloted planes crashed.

Clément Ader

In 1897, Ader's plane the *Avion No. 3* flew 300 feet before crashing.

Ader built the plane's propellers from bamboo. The plane was covered with fabric.

Flying!

The Wright brothers wore suits, even when flying.

Orville and Wilbur Wright

Wilbur and Orville Wright * flipped a coin in December 1903. Wilbur won. He climbed into the brothers' gas-engine propeller plane. *The Flyer* shot down the starter track, went a few feet in the air — and crashed. A few days later, it was Orville's turn. On December 17, he took off from Kitty Hawk, North Carolina — into aviation history! Orville stayed in the air for 12 seconds. *The Flyer* traveled 120 feet. It was the world's first piloted, powered, controlled, sustained flight. The Wright brothers were successful because they understood that flying machines, like bicycles, had to stay balanced as they moved.

The Flyer's wing coverings were made from cotton. ❑ ▼

Early airplane wings had wooden frames.

The engine and bicycle chains turned the propellers in opposite directions to keep the plane balanced in flight.

▲ The curved propellers were made of sprucewood.

The Flyer's starting track was a 60-foot wooden rail. ▶

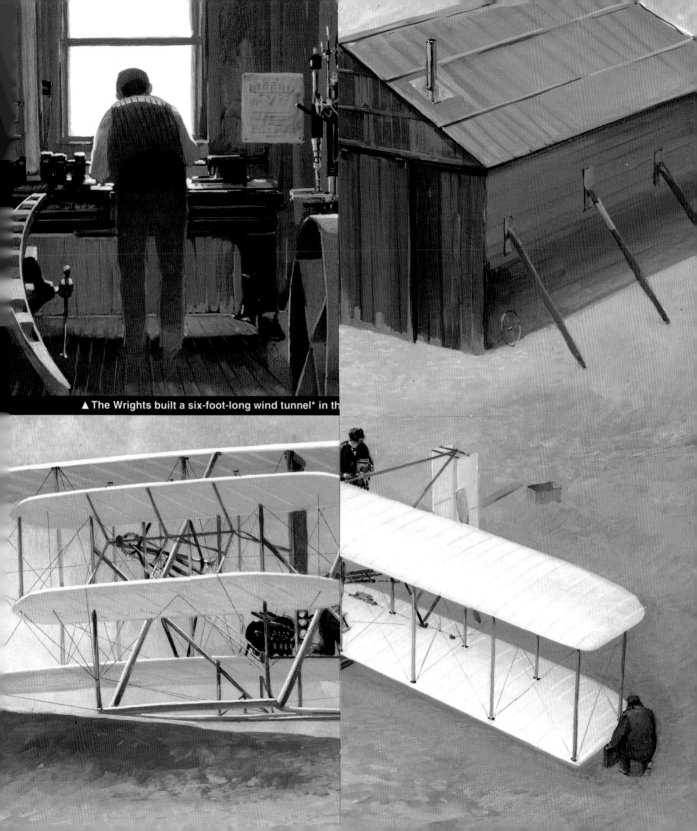

▲ The Wrights built a six-foot-long wind tunnel* in th

Ace Pilots

1

The first aviators were inventors, entertainers, and pilots all in one. The newspapers were full of their adventures and their accidents. In 1927, **Charles Lindbergh*** crossed the Atlantic—alone and nonstop! The brave pilot boarded the *Spirit of St. Louis* in New York in a rainstorm on the morning of May 20. The single-engine plane landed 33 hours and 39 minutes later near Paris, France, on the evening of May 21. "Lucky Lindy" was the world's hero!

a

1. Alberto Santos-Dumont's *Demoiselle*. The first *Demoiselle* flew in November 1907. The design was built in modest numbers, and each plane was constructed by hand.

On July 25, 1909, French aviator Louis Blériot won a newspaper contest by becoming the first person to cross the English Channel from France to England in a heavier-than-air aircraft.

Blériot's 23.5-mile trip took about 37 minutes. ▶

2. Men steady a plane while the engine starts.
3. Airmail stamps honor early aviation. ❏
4. Planes began to fly everywhere.

4

d

a. Louis Blériot
b. Harriet Quimby
c. Charles Lindbergh
d. Antoine de Saint-Exupéry

The *Spirit of St. Louis*

The *Spirit of St. Louis* was built in two months. The cockpit* was only 37 inches wide and 51 inches high. Charles Lindbergh sat inside in a wicker chair. He used a periscope to see forward. He also kept the side windows open; when he felt sleepy, he stuck out his head. The cold air woke him up. Lindbergh didn't carry a radio or parachute, so there would be more room for fuel. The historic flight covered 3,610 miles. The plane flew 100 mph, at altitudes from 50 to 10,000 feet.

Spirited Aviators

In 1912, Harriet Quimby* became the first woman to fly across the English Channel. Antoine de Saint-Exupéry*, the famous pilot and author of *The Little Prince* (1943), helped start overseas airmail in the 1920s. Bessie Coleman* became the first African-American woman to get a pilot's license (1921). Amelia Earhart* crossed the Atlantic alone in 1932.

Flying Boats

Pan Am clippers were luxurious seaplanes

The *Philippine Clipper* (1935)

that could cross the Pacific Ocean.

Lindbergh lands at Le Bourget airport. French officials protect him from the crowd of 100,000. ▼

Warplanes

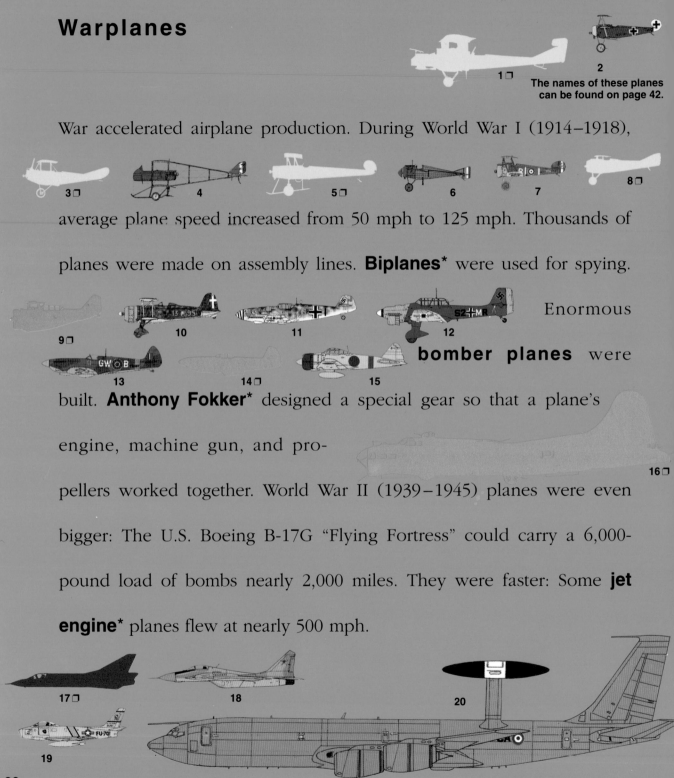

The names of these planes can be found on page 42.

War accelerated airplane production. During World War I (1914–1918), average plane speed increased from 50 mph to 125 mph. Thousands of planes were made on assembly lines. **Biplanes*** were used for spying. Enormous **bomber planes** were built. **Anthony Fokker*** designed a special gear so that a plane's engine, machine gun, and pro-pellers worked together. World War II (1939–1945) planes were even bigger: The U.S. Boeing B-17G "Flying Fortress" could carry a 6,000-pound load of bombs nearly 2,000 miles. They were faster: Some **jet engine*** planes flew at nearly 500 mph.

2. German BMW 801 radial engine used during World War II. Its cylinders stayed in place. The crankshaft in the middle spins.

3. French SNECMA M 88 jet engine used today. A jet engine burns fuel and air to help push the plane forward.

At the Controls

The pilot pulls the joystick back to raise the elevators and make the plane climb. The elevators are like horizontal tail rudders. ❑

A pilot runs the plane's control system with a hand-powered **joystick*** or steering wheel and foot-powered **rudder pedals***. The pilot needs both controls to adjust the plane's angle and direction. The pilot pushes on the rudder pedals to steer with the vertical rudder (shown in pink). Pulling on the joystick or wheel moves the pitch control surfaces or elevators (orange) and the **ailerons*** (blue). The plane is tilted by raising or lowering the ailerons and turning the rudder. The pilot can slow down or speed up by using the **gas throttle**, which controls the engine's power.

To turn right, the pilot pushes the joystick to the right and presses down on the rudder pedal with the right foot.

Without a tail rotor*, a helicopter would spin around like a top.

Rotor ▲

Tail rotor ▶

Helicopter Flight

Helicopter blades are the same shape as airplane wings. But helicopter blades are not fixed like wings. They spin very quickly. The rotating blades lift, propel, and help steer the helicopter. Because its blades are constantly turning, a

Veering left ❑

helicopter can hover. It can take off vertically and fly backward, sideways, or turn around.

▲ **Robinson R 44 helicopter (1990)**

Chopper Power!

Helicopters are often used in rescues because they can hover, land, or take off in places where a plane could not. Choppers are also used for traffic reporting and air taxis!

Climbing

Hovering ❑

Descent

▲ **Changing the blade angle changes the flight direction.**

To dive, the pilot pushes the joystick forward. The elevators go down. ❑

◀ **The plane travels in a straight line before landing.**

Takeoff and Landing

A plane takes off and lands heading into the wind, just as a bird does. This way the speed of the wind does not increase the speed of the plane.

Before Landing

A plane's speed increases as it descends. The pilot uses the control system to slow down. The right speed is important. Too slow a speed will stall a plane.

To make the plane tilt to the right, the pilot pushes the joystick to the right. The right aileron (blue) comes up and the left aileron goes down.

Navigation

An aerial navigation chart showing the range of radio beacons.

Flight involves navigation or planning a route. Navigators have to think about direction, speed, and wind. Early pilots used compasses and **maps**. They also checked their courses using landmarks and stars. In the 1920s, **radio beacons** showed the plane's exact position. In the late 1930s, the use of **radar*** became more common. Today, most flight information is computerized.

Pilots once wore leather coats, gloves, and fur-lined boots to protect themselves against the cold or bad weather.

Airbus A340

The radar screen shows weather action, wind speed and direction, aircraft speed, and the distance to the next radio beacon.

Flight Check

All the flight instruments are checked before takeoff. When the plane is airborne, the pilot can put it on automatic pilot. A computer will monitor and adjust the course.

Flight Instruments

Flight instruments help the pilot guide the plane. The altimeter measures altitude or flying height. The airspeed indicator measures speed. The artificial horizon shows the flying angle during a turn. The directional gyroscope helps keep the plane on a straight course. The information from these and other flight instruments shows up on electronic screens in a modern cockpit.

Navigation Instruments

The most important navigational tool is the VOR/VHF Omnidirectional Range, a radio-guidance apparatus that transmits the signals from the radio beacons and radar.

Alpha, Bravo...

The pilot uses a radio to communicate with air traffic control centers and with other airplanes in flight. An international phonetic alphabet (*see* page 42) is used for radio messages from the cockpit.

The Engines

Dials and gauges in the cockpit display information about the engines and fuel use.

At high speeds, blood rushes quickly to the head or feet. An anti-G* suit protects pilots from this painful effect.

Now Boarding...

McDonnell-Douglas DC-10

After World War I, some bomber planes were changed into **passenger planes***. These planes made the first international flights, from Paris to London, in 1919. They carried 11 passengers. In 1936, 21-passenger planes flew from New York to Los Angeles in about 18 hours. Then jet engines were built. By the late 1950s, up to 112 passengers could cross the United States in four to six hours. Today's jumbo jets can carry nearly 500 people at speeds of 608 mph.

Jet planes fly at high altitudes to avoid bad weather and conserve fuel.

The Concorde was the first supersonic* passenger jet. Its initial flight was in March 1969. It can fly 1,000 mph and cross the Atlantic Ocean in less than three hours.

Pressurization

A Boeing 747 flies at an altitude of 30,000 feet, where the air is thin. Air pressure inside the plane has to be normal, so that passengers can breathe. During the flight, fresh air from outside the plane is sucked in by a pump and then circulated inside the fuselage* or main body of the plane. This is called pressurization.

◄ The area where passengers sit is called the cabin. The ailerons of a Boeing 747 adjust during the different phases of the flight. ▼

Supersonic Hero

Planes that came close to the speed of sound often went out of control—and sometimes crashed. Many people thought a plane could never be supersonic or move faster than sound. Brigadier General Charles "Chuck" Yeager*, U.S. Air Force, proved them wrong. In 1947, he flew a small, orange, rocket-powered plane 660 mph — fast enough to break the sound barrier! Yeager's plane, the Bell X-1 "Glamorous Glennis," was shaped like a bullet to help it reach top speed.

Sonic Boom

When a jet travels at supersonic speeds, it causes a shock wave in the air. This wave is heard as a loud, exploding sonic boom. Supersonic speeds are measured in Mach* numbers.

FLY
ANYWHERE ANY TIME
CURTISS
CURTISS FLYING SERVICE

U.S. aviator Glenn Curtiss won the first International Aviation Competition in 1909. Then he started his own plane manufacturing company and flying service.

Planes of the Future

Aerodynamic engineers are working on jet
planes and rocket planes that will travel
farther and faster. Research into **VTOL**
(vertical takeoff and landing) and **STOL**
(short takeoff and landing) aircraft could change
air routes and airports worldwide. Hovercrafts that
move by floating on fan-generated cushions of air are
already in use. Scientists are experimenting with new
lightweight materials for plane construction. It might be electronically
possible to build a **smart wing**. A computerized wing like this could
"think" and "respond" to changing flight conditions. Then there's *space*
flight. Wouldn't Leonardo da Vinci
be amazed!

The Northrop B-2 (1989) has a two-seat cockpit and a special coating that interferes with radar waves. This stealth bomber is hard to track!

A heads-up display helmet puts all the flight information right in front of the pilot's eyes.

Cockpits of the future may have touch- or voice-activated control screens.

The Bell/Boeing V-22 "Osprey" (1989) flies like a plane, but can take off and land vertically, like a helicopter.

Computer drawing of an unducted fan: a jet equipped with a new type of propeller

The Alliance

The Alliance is in the concept stage. It will travel at 1,400 mph and fly 7,500 miles without refueling. The Alliance is being designed to carry 250 passengers. They should be able to board in the year 2010!

Vertical Takeoff and Landing

If jets could take off and land like helicopters, they wouldn't need such long runways. But helicopters cannot fly very fast. Engineers are testing jets with rotors that swivel, like the Bell/Boeing V-22 "Osprey." This would allow for VTOL *and* speed.

Rocket-Powered Planes

These planes would take off horizontally; their engines would use the oxygen in the atmosphere. Once in space, they would operate like rockets. Rocket-powered planes would be able to travel at Mach 25. They would make the nearly 12,000-mile trip from London, England, to Sydney, Australia, in just two hours!

Supersonic-Turboram Jet Combos!

Aircraft capable of flight in both the earth's atmosphere and in space will combine several means of propulsion: turbojets* for takeoff, ram jets for supersonic speed, and rocket engines for space flight.

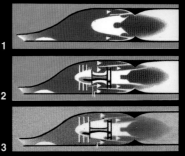

1. Rocket engine and ram jet engine
2. Turboram rocket
3. Ram rocket ❐

This hypersonic plane should be able to reach a speed of Mach 5! ▼

MCDONNELL DOUGLAS

"*I owned the world that hour as I rode over it…free of the earth, free of the mountains, free of the clouds, but how inseparably I was bound to them.*"

Charles Lindbergh

(1902–1974) U.S. aviator
From Leonard Mosely, *Lindbergh*
(New York: Doubleday, 1978)

◀ A model of the Concorde in a water tunnel. Colored fluids show the flow of air.

Index

Time Line

	Prehistory/Antiquity 2 million B.C.–A.D. 476	**Middle Ages** A.D. 476–1492	**Renaissance** 1492–1600
Flight	**250 million years ago** First dragonflies **150 million years ago** First birds, like archaeopteryx **1000 B.C.** Greek myth of Icarus and Daedalus **400 B.C.** Chinese invent the kite	**ca. 1020** Eilmer de Malmesbury, the "flying monk," makes himself wings and leaps from a tower of the abbey—he breaks his legs **ca. 1200** Chinese develop first rockets **ca. 1250** Roger Bacon, another monk, designs a balloon **ca. 1295** Marco Polo reports men flying on kites in China	**ca. 1486–1506** Leonardo da Vinci designs and builds models of birdlike flying machines
Science and Nature	**1.8 million years ago** First stone tools **500,000 B.C.** Taming of fire **40,000 B.C.** Ice Age ends **ca. 3500 B.C.** First known use of wheels in Sumeria **1800 B.C.** Babylonians invent multiplication tables **A.D. 79** Mount Vesuvius erupts and buries Pompeii	**ca. 500** Mathematicians in India invent the zero and decimal numbers **868** First book printed in China with carved woodblocks **1030** First school of medicine established in Salerno, Italy **1438** Johannes Gutenberg invents the printing press	**1509–1590** Ambroise Paré, father of modern surgery **1543** Death of Nicolaus Copernicus, who believed the earth and the rest of the universe revolve around the sun **1590** Compound microscope invented
Visual Arts	**ca. 15,000 B.C.** Lascaux cave paintings **ca. 3000 B.C.** Stonehenge built in England **ca. 1500 B.C.** Egyptian papyrus **221–210 B.C.** Construction of the Great Wall of China **ca. 200–190 B.C.** *Nike of Samothrace*	**1067** First panel of Bayeux tapestry woven in France **ca. 1100** Gothic style of architecture is introduced in Europe **1174– ca. 1350** Tower of Pisa constructed **1266–1337** Giotto, Italian painter **ca. 1440–1450** Fra Angelico's *The Annunciation*	**ca. 1500** Sandro Botticelli's *The Nativity* **ca. 1503–1505** Leonardo da Vinci's *Mona Lisa* **1508–1512** Michelangelo paints the ceiling of the Sistine Chapel **1510–1511** Raphael's *The School of Athens*
Music and Theater	**ca. 60,000 B.C.** First flutes, made out of bone **ca. 3000 B.C.** Lyres and harps in Mesopotamia **ca. 450 B.C.** Birth of Greek theater	**1026** Guido d'Arezzo names the musical notes (do, re, mi, etc.) **1100s** The troubadour tradition of secular songs and poems develops in southern France **1200s** The rise of Chinese drama	**1500s** Major and minor scales are developed **ca. 1550** First performances of the commedia dell'arte in Italy **1572** Andrea Amati makes the first violoncello **1576** First British public theater opens near London
Literature	**ca. 3250 B.C.** Invention of writing **1100** Pa-out-She, Chinese scholar, compiles first dictionary **ca. 1000 B.C.** Oldest books of the Old Testament are written down **ca. 800 B.C.** Homer's *Iliad* and *Odyssey* **414 B.C.** Aristophanes' *The Birds*	**618–907** Greatest Chinese poets: Li Bo and Du Fu **ca. 1000** *Beowulf* **Early 1000s** Murasaki Shikibu's *The Tale of Genji*, Japanese novel **1321** Dante's *The Divine Comedy* **1387–1400** Geoffrey Chaucer's *The Canterbury Tales*	**1532–1534** Francois Rabelais's *Gargantua and Pantagruel* **1590–1596** Edmund Spenser's *The Faerie Queen* **1594** William Shakespeare's *Romeo and Juliet*
History	**1361–1352 B.C.** Egyptian boy king Tutankhamen reigns **ca. 500 B.C.** Buddhism founded in India **ca. 6 B.C.–A.D. 30** Jesus Christ	**476** Fall of the Roman Empire **ca. 600** Islam religion founded in Arabia **1325** Tenochtitlán, capital of the Aztec empire, founded	**late 1400s** Incas build walled city of Machu Picchu **1492** Christopher Columbus lands in the Bahamas **1517** Martin Luther's Reformation begins

17th Century	18th Century	19th Century	20th Century

1687 Sir Isaac Newton discovers law of universal gravitation

1783 The Montgolfier brothers launch their first hot-air balloon at Annonay, France
1783 Jacques-Alexandre-César Charles and Nicolas and Anne-Jean Robert launch the first hydrogen-filled balloon—Benjamin Franklin witnesses the event
1797 First parachute descent from a balloon by André-Jacques Garnerin

1852 First airship flight
1853 Sir George Cayley builds the first man-carrying glider
1858 Gaspard-Félix Tournachon becomes the world's first aerial photographer, shooting pictures from a balloon
1891 Otto Lilienthal makes his first glider flight
1897 Clément Ader's *Avion No. 3* gets off the ground

1903 The Wright brothers' first flight
1914 First aerial combat
1918 First U.S. airmail service
1927 Charles Lindbergh's solo nonstop transatlantic flight
1932 Amelia Earhart's solo non-stop transatlantic flight
1969 First Concorde flight
1994 Astronauts use jet packs to free-fly in space

1609 Galileo constructs first of his many telescopes
1612 Italian physician Sanctorius invents first clinical thermometer
1656 First pendulum clock made by Christiaan Huygens
1663 Danish physician Nicolaus Steno demonstrates that the heart is a muscle

1735 Swedish botanist Carolus Linnaeus invents a classification system for animals and plants
1743–1794 Antoine-Laurent Lavoisier, the founder of modern chemistry
1752 Benjamin Franklin invents the lightning rod
1793 Eli Whitney invents the cotton gin

1803 Richard Trevithick builds first steam railway locomotive
1844 Samuel F. B. Morse begins first telegraph service
1876 Alexander Graham Bell patents the telephone
1879 Thomas Edison invents the electric lightbulb
1885 Louis Pasteur develops a vaccine against rabies

1905 Albert Einstein formulates the theory of relativity: $E = mc^2$
1928 Sir Alexander Fleming discovers penicillin
1945 First atomic bomb
1948 First computer developed
1950 Color television
1969 Neil Armstrong walks on the moon
1970 Compact disk developed

1609 Peter Paul Rubens's *Adoration of the Magi*
ca. 1631–1645 Taj Mahal constructed in northern India
1642 Rembrandt's *The Night Watch*
1661 French King Louis XIV begins construction of the palace of Versailles

1700s The age of portraiture
1765 John Singleton Copley's *Boy with a Squirrel*
1793 Gilbert Stuart's *George Washington*

1800s Landscape woodblock prints by Hokusai and Hiroshige popular in Japan
1860s Birth of Impressionism in France
1880 Mary Cassatt's *Young Mother Sewing*
1889 Vincent van Gogh's *Starry Night*

1919 Constantin Brancusi's *Bird in Space*
1929 Empire State Building constructed in New York City
1931 Georgia O'Keeffe's *Cow's Skull with Calico Roses*
1937 Pablo Picasso's *Guernica*
1962 Andy Warhol's *The Twenty Marilyns*

---

ca. 1600 Tang Xianzu's *The Peony Pavilion*
ca. 1600 Japanese develop Kabuki theater
1643 Molière establishes his theater troupe in France
1644–1737 Antonio Stradivari, considered maker of finest violins
1678–1741 Antonio Vivaldi, Italian violinist and composer

1722 Johann Sebastian Bach's *The Well-Tempered Clavier*
1725 Antonio Vivaldi's *The Four Seasons*
1749 George Frideric Handel's *Fireworks Music*
1787 Wolfgang Amadeus Mozart's *Eine kleine Nachtmusik*

1824 Ludwig van Beethoven's *Ninth Symphony*
1841 Richard Wagner's *Der fliegende Holländer*
1892 Pyotr Ilich Tchaikovsky's *The Nutcracker*

ca. 1900 Birth of jazz
1928 Walt Disney releases first animated *Mickey Mouse* cartoon
1936 Sergei Prokofief's *Peter and the Wolf*
1939 *The Wizard of Oz*
1955 Beginnings of rock and roll
1960 Invention of the synthesizer
1963 Alfred Hitchcock's *The Birds*

1600–1601 William Shakespeare's *Hamlet*
1605 Miguel de Cervantes's *Don Quixote*
ca. 1612–1672 Anne Bradstreet, early American poet
1667 John Milton's *Paradise Lost*
1678 John Bunyan's *Pilgrim's Progress*

1700s Lao Xueqin's *The Story of the Stone* (greatest Chinese novel)
1719 Daniel Defoe's *Robinson Crusoe*
1726 Jonathan Swift's *Gulliver's Travels*

1809–1849 Edgar Allan Poe
1863 Jules Verne's *Five Weeks in a Balloon*
1865 Lewis Carroll's *Alice's Adventures in Wonderland*
1868 Louisa May Alcott's *Little Women*
1884 Mark Twain's *The Adventures of Huckleberry Finn*

1908 Kenneth Grahame's *The Wind in the Willows*
1932 Laura Ingalls Wilder's *Little House in the Big Woods*
1937 J. R. R. Tolkien's *The Hobbit*
1952 E. B. White's *Charlotte's Web*

1607 English settlers establish Jamestown Colony in Virginia
1620 Pilgrims land at Plymouth Rock
1682–1725 Czar Peter the Great reigns in Russia

1773 Boston Tea Party
1776 U.S. Declaration of Independence signed
1789 George Washington elected first U.S. president
1789–1799 French Revolution

1831 British explorer James Ross finds North Magnetic Pole
1846–1847 Irish potato famine
1861–1865 U.S. Civil War
1899–1900 Boxer Rebellion in China

1914–1918 World War I
1917–1922 Russian Revolution
1939–1945 World War II
1945 The birth of the United Nations
1989 Fall of the Berlin Wall

Illustrators

P. Biard: **12b, 12rc, 13 (die cut overlay recto and verso), 13rc, 13tm, 13b**
J.-P. Chabot: **8tr, 8b, 9, 16lc-16br**
L. Favreau: **27b**
A. Kinsey: **21t (br four-part foldout verso)**
P. Mitschké: **20, 21, 21m (tl four-part foldout verso), 21b (tr four-part foldout verso), 21m (br four-part foldout verso)**
D. Moignot: **22–23 (diagrams of the rudder bar and joystick), 24l, 24b, 25 (die cut overlays I–II recto and verso), 25tl, 25bl, 25br**
J.-M. Poissenot: **4b, 5, 10tl, 10bl, 10mr, 10br, 19mr**
M. Pommier: **inside front cover, 31–46**
J. Prunier: **14b, 15t, 15b, 17, 18b, 19b (acetate overlay recto and verso), 19b (bl four-part foldout verso), 21 (br four-part foldout verso), 22t, 22b, 23, 26t**
E. Souppart: **28, 29tl, 29ml, 29b, 29mr**
P.-M. Valat: **cover, 2m, 3m (die cut overlay recto and verso), 3m, 6bl, 6br (after A. Magnan), 7tl, 7ml, 7bl, 7br, 11, 14tr** (after a drawing excerpted from the work of Otto Lilienthal, *Der Vogelflug als Grundlage der Fliegekunst*, ca. 1890), **26b**

Credits

All Rights Reserved: **19tl**
Bibliothèque Nationale, Paris, France: **2br, 3tr, 19tr (acetate overlay verso)**
British Airways, Paris-La Défense, France: **27t**
J. L. Charmet, Paris, France (Special Collection): **12tr**
Curtiss-Wright Corporation, Lyndhurst, NJ: **7r**
Gallimard Jeunesse, Paris, France (Photo P. Léger): **16bl, 16bm, 24tr**
Francisco Goya y Lucientes, *The Kite*, 1779, Museo del Prado, Madrid, Spain/Giraudon, Paris, France: **8tl**
Henry Groskinsky, New York, NY: **3mr**
Illustration by J.-M. Guillou/All Rights Reserved: **12tl**
Jacana, Vanves, France (Photo D. Manfred): **7mr**
Keystone, Paris, France: **13tr, 13mr**
Leonardo da Vinci, "Experiment on Lifting Power of Wing," 1490–1493, *Ms. B*, folio 88 verso, Bibliothèque de l'Institut de France, Paris, France/Bulloz, Paris, France: **3t (die cut overlay verso)**
Leonardo da Vinci, "The Flight of Birds," *Codex Volo Uccelli*, 1505–1515, folio 7 verso, Biblioteca Reale di Torino, Turin, Italy: **3t (die cut overlay recto), 3b (die cut overlay recto)**
Leonardo da Vinci, "Wing for Spring-Operated Machine," 1490–1493, *Codex Atlanticus*, folio 308 recto-a, Biblioteca Ambrosiana, Milan, Italy: **3b (die cut overlay verso)**
Musée Air France, Paris, France: **19tr**
Musée de l'Air et de l'Espace, Le Bourget, France: **3m (die cut overlay verso)–3m** (colored by Laure Massin), **3tr, 14ml, 15mr, 18tl, 19tl (acetate overlay recto), 19tr (acetate overlay recto), 21 (tl four-part foldout recto), 21 (tr four-part foldout recto), 21tr (tl four-part foldout verso), 21ml (tr four-part foldout verso), 21 tr (tr four-part foldout verso), 26tr**
Musée de la Poste, Paris, France: **19tl (acetate overlay verso)**
Musées Royaux des Beaux-Arts de Belgique, Brussels, Belgium/Giraudon, Vanves, France: **2bl**
Museo Leonardino, Vinci, Italy: **3bl**
NASA, Washington, DC: **29tr**
Natural History Photo Agency, Ardingly, Sussex, England/Sunset, Paris, France: **7m**
C. Nurisdany and M. Pérennou, Paris, France: **4lc**
Onera, Châtillon, France: **30**
Quadrant Picture Library, Surrey, England: **25tr**
Smithsonian Institution, Washington, DC: **16tr, 18tr**
Snecma, Paris, France: **21 (bl four-part foldout recto), 21 (br four-part foldout recto)**
Sunset, Paris, France (Photo G. Lacz): **6t, 6m**
Sygma, Paris, France (Photo L'Illustration): **13br**
Jules Verne, *Cinq Semaines en Ballon*, illustrated by Riou (Paris, France: Editions Hetzel), ca. 1863/All Rights Reserved: **10tr**

Acknowledgments

Aérospatiale, Paris, France.
Airbus Industrie, Toulouse-Blagnac, France.
Air France and Musée Air France, Paris, France.
John Amrhein, Northrop Corp., Los Angeles, CA.
Anacostia Naval Air Station, Washington, DC.
Terry A. Arnold, Bell Helicopter Textron, Hurst, T
Robert A. Bosi, Curtiss-Wright Corporation, Lyndhurst, NJ.
British Airways, Paris-La Défense, France.
David Burgevin and Brian Nicklas, Smithsonian Institution, Washington, DC.
Madelyne Busch, Boeing Defense & Space, Philadelphia, PA.
Eurocopter, Paris, France.
Richard Fenwick, Paris, France.
Don Hanson, McDonnell Douglas Aircraft Co., McDonnell Douglas Corp., Long Beach, CA.
Constance Moore, NASA, Washington, DC.
Musée Air France, Paris, France.
Musée de l'Air et de l'Espace, Le Bourget, France.
Alexandra Rose, iconographer, New York, NY.
Snecma, Paris, France.
Anne-Catherine Souchon, journalist, Paris, France.

Have you found the right spot for each sticker?
Numbers 1, 24: page 19 / 2, 3, 5, 6, 8, 10–12: page 20 / 4, 7, 9: page 21 / 13: page 13 / 14: page 10 / 16: page 24 / 15, 17, 18, 21–23, 27, 31, 32: page 25 / 19: page 9 / 20: page 4 / 25: page 2 / 26, 29, 33: page 23 / 28: page 22 / 30: page 29 / 34: page 16

SCHOLASTIC
VOYAGES
OF DISCOVERY™

Natural History Exploring Space Trees and Forests Wind and Weather	**Science and Technology** Taming Fire Exploring Energy The Story of Flight
Visual Arts Paint and Painting The Art of Sculpture Architecture and Construction	**Music and Performing Arts** Musical Instruments The World of Theater The History of Movie Making

Key:
l = left **b** = bottom
r = right **m** = middle
t = top **c** = column